The Fort
in the
Wilderness

Katherine M. Strobeck

Illustrations by
Emerson Lamb

North Country Books
Utica, New York

THE FORT IN THE WILDERNESS

ISBN 0-925168-62-9

First Hardcover Printing 1978
First Paperback Printing 1998

*North Country Books thanks Marine Midland Bank
for permission to reproduce the painting by Tom Lotta,
"Fort Stanwix—The Stronghold that Wouldn't Surrender,"
as part of the cover, and for use of the diagram
of the fort and glossary of technical terms.
A special thanks to David Veeder for the original drawing
of the Mohawk Valley during the Revolutionary War.
Our sincere thanks to the National Park Service
for valuable help in checking the accuracy of
historical references in "The Fort in the Wilderness."*

\

North Country Books, Inc.
311 Turner Street
Utica, New York 13501

To my friends
of the Glenville Hills,
lineal descendants of
Jan Van Epps

Jedediah Quackenbush is a fictional character.
For the most part, the events and the other people in this
book are based on actual events and real people.

During the Revolutionary War, Fort Stanwix was known as Fort Schuyler. Built by the British during the French and Indian War, the fort was named after General John Stanwix, the commanding British officer of the area. The British abandoned the fort after the war and it fell into disrepair. At the beginning of the revolution the Americans rebuilt the fort and renamed it Fort Schuyler after General Philip Schuyler, the commanding American officer of the area. Known as Fort Schuyler for only a few years, the fort reverted to its original name which is used throughout this narrative.

The Mohawk Valley during the Revolutionary War

N

Creek

Johnstown

Stone Arabia

Ft. Johnson

Ft. Hunter

Mohawk River

Canajoharie

Sharon Springs

ld

he.ry Valley

Schenectady

Schoharie

Albany

Middleburg
(Middle Fort)

Upper Fort

Hudson River

David Vorder 1997

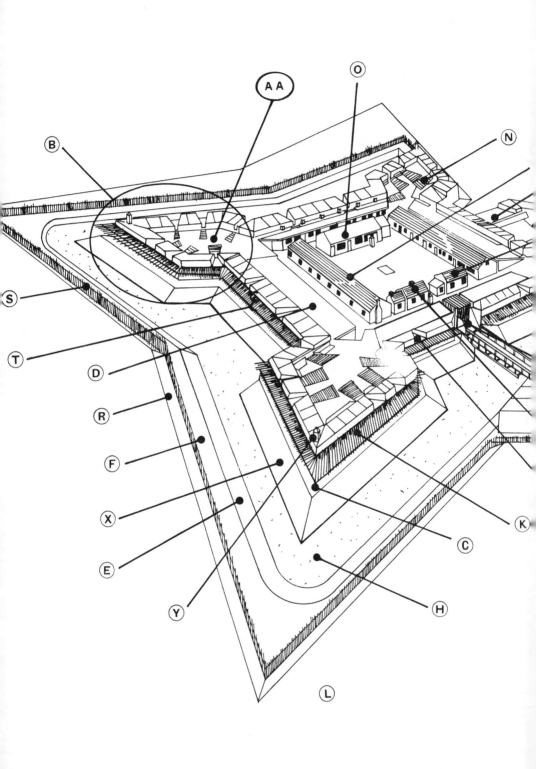

A Listing and Glossary of Technical Terms

Keyed to a diagram of Fort Stanwix

A. BARRACKS: " . . . places erected for both officers and men to lodge in; they are built different ways, according to their different situations. When there is sufficient room to make a large square, surrounded with buildings, they are very convenient. . . ."

B. BASTION: ". . . a part of the inner inclosure of a fortification, making an angle towards the field, and consists of 2 faces, 2 flanks, and an opening towards the centre of the place. . . ."

C. BERM: ". . . a little space, or path of 6 or 8 feet broad, between the ditch and talus of the parapet; it is to prevent the earth from rolling into the ditch. . . ."

D. CASEMATE: A structure built into the ramparts with a reinforced roof to protect troops. Used as barracks at Fort Stanwix.

E. COUNTERSCARP: ". . . the exterior talus, or slope, of the ditch. . . ."

F. COVERED WAY: ". . . is a space . . . going quite around the works, and is adjoined to the counterscarp of the ditches, covered by a parapet. . . ."

G. CURTAIN WALL: ". . . is that part of the body of the place which joins the flank of one bastion to that of another. . . ."

H. DITCH: ". . . a large deep trench made round each work , . . the dirt dug out of it serves to raise the rampart and parapet. . . ."

I. DRAWBRIDGE: A hinged section of bridge that can be drawn up to prevent access to entrance of fort.

J. EMBRASURE: ". . . an opening, hole, or aperture in a parapet, through which the cannon are pointed to fire at the enemy. . . ."

K. FRAISE: ". . . palisades placed horizontally on the outward slope of a rampart . . . to prevent the work being taken by surprise. . . ."

L. GLACIS: ". . . is the part beyond the (covered way), to which it serves as a parapet and terminates toward the Field in an easy slope. . . ."

M. GUARD HOUSE: A place for the off-duty guards to sleep during their tour of duty and where prisoners were sometimes kept.

N. GUN PLATFORM: A wooden platform to support the weight of cannon.

O. HEADQUARTERS BUILDING: The quarters of the ranking officers and where orders were issued.

P. NECESSARY: The privy or outhouse.

Q. PARAPET: ". . . an elevation . . . designed for covering the soldiers from the enemy's cannon, or small shot. . . ."

R. PARAPET OF GLACIS: A parapet between the glacis and the Covered Way, on the outside of the Picket Line.

S. PICKET LINE: ". . . stakes made of strong split wood, about 9 feet long, fixed 3 feet deep in the ground, in rows about 6 inches asunder; they are placed in the (covered way). . . ."

T. RAMPART: ". . . an elevation of earth raised along the faces of any work, of 10 or 15 feet high, to cover the inner part of that work against the fire of an enemy. . . ."

U. RAVELIN: ". . . works raised on the counterscarp before the curtain of the place, and serve to cover the gates . . . and the bridges. They consist of two faces forming a (salient) angle and are defended by the faces of the neighboring bastions. . . ."

V. REDOUBT: A detached work surrounded by a parapet to guard a weak point in the defenses.

W. SALLY PORT: ". . . are those underground passages, which lead from the inner works to the outward ones. . . . When they are made for men to go through only, they are made with steps at the entrance, and going out. . . ."

X. SCARP: ". . . the interior talus or slope of the ditch next (to) the place, at the foot of the rampart. . . ."

Y. SENTRY BOX: A little house to keep a sentinel dry in wet weather.

Z. STORE HOUSE: Used to store clothing, bedding, and some food.

AA. TERREPLEIN: ". . . the top platform, or horizontal surface of the rampart, whereon the cannon are placed, as well as the troops that defend the place. . . ."

All quoted definitions have been taken from Captain George Smith's *Universal Military Dictionary*, published in 1779.

The Campaign

The summer of 1777 found the British embarked on a bold scheme to crush the Colonists and end the American Revolution.

Burgoyne, marching from Montreal by way of Lake Champlain, was to capture Fort Ticonderoga and proceed to Albany.

St. Leger, coming from Oswego through Oneida Lake and Wood Creek, needed only to subdue Fort Stanwix. The way would then be open for him to sweep down the Mohawk Valley.

Lord Howe would come up the Hudson River from New York City.

The three armies were to meet in Albany. With New York cut off from New England, the young Republic might not survive.

CHAPTER ONE

The Mohawk War Trail

Jed Quackenbush hadn't realized he was running through the silent Mohawk Valley woods until Jan called to him.

"What's the matter?" Jan Van Epps panted. "Are you scared of something?"

"No!" Jed, his dark eyes narrowing, hoped he was telling the truth. "I don't like the looks of this trail. Only a well-used Indian trail would be worn as deep as this. We'd better leave it and follow the creek down to the river and the Kingsroad. Want to rest a minute?"

Jan gratefully unhooked the tall regimental drum slung over his shoulder. The boys had been traveling all day from Jed's farm home at Stone Arabia, fifteen miles north of the Mohawk River in central New York. The sun was hot that August day in 1777.

"Phew," he said, rubbing his shoulders where the drum straps had cut into his linen shirt. "I thought we were going to run the whole way to Fort Stanwix. We'd be there ahead of the British and Americans both."

"We've got to get to Fort Dayton tomorrow." Jed, normally an easygoing farm boy, was tense and impatient. "All the Mohawk Valley regiments are meeting there to march to Fort Stanwix to stop the British. Colonel Klock, the commander of the Palatine Regiment knows me. He'll let me join."

"You're right," Jan answered. "I don't suppose they'll wait for me either even though I am such a good drummer."

With Jed's musket close at hand, the two boys lay flat on the bank and let cold water run through their mouths. Jed, at fifteen, was tall and dark haired, dressed in a homespun shirt and buckskin breeches. Jan, the younger of the two, showed his Dutch ancestry clearly in his bright blue eyes and butter colored hair.

Jan started to rise but Jed clutched his shoulder.

"Keep down," he whispered, "don't move. Hear that bluejay calling. Someone is behind us. We'd better get under that windfall."

Across the creek a thick hemlock had come down in a storm.

"Walk in the water," Jed cautioned. "If you step on a stone, it will leave a wet spot."

The bushes parted. Jed gasped, forcing himself to lie still.

"Mohawks," he breathed in Jan's ear, "in warpaint. Scouts for the British, probably."

Four Indians with bars of black and white streaked across their faces and arms trotted to the edge of the stream. Leather leggings covered the lower halves of their bodies; their upper halves glistened with oil. They were Mohawks, one of the six tribes of the Iroquois Confederacy, once the most powerful political organization in North America. Although scattered now by the white man's greed for land, wars, and unfavorable treaties, a few pockets of Mohawks remained in the valley. Of the remaining Iroquois tribes, only the Oneidas and Tuscaroras befriended the colonists.

Jed's teeth chattered, although sweat poured from his face. Painted Mohawks on the war trail meant deadly trouble.

Stiff scalp locks, heavy with grease, rose from the tops of their shaved heads. Tomahawks and scalping knives

swayed as they knelt to drink.

Two were kneeling at the stream, but as the third bent over, his head jerked up. Fierce black eyes stared as a fern, crushed as the boys lay down to drink, slowly straightened up. All four were on their feet now, pointing to the fern and the brush along the bank.

Only the leader had not drawn his tomahawk. Standing close to where the boys crouched, he pointed north and strode away. Two of the savages followed, but the fourth came directly to the windfall, poking and jabbing with his tomahawk. Soon he was slashing at the branches hiding the boys.

The leader came back, barking a sharp command. The disgruntled Mohawk lopped off one more branch before he turned and followed.

Jed counted fifty breaths before he dared raise his head. Little remained of their shelter.

"Were they a war party?" Jan's blue eyes showed almost black in his round white face.

"I don't think so." Jed's knees were trembling as he pulled himself up. "A war party would be larger and probably headed south. I think they are going to Fort Stanwix to meet St. Leger and the British and help them capture the fort. They were in a real hurry about something. They knew we were close by."

They soon reached the Kingsroad along the Mohawk River, the main route west from Albany and Schenectady, and slept that night at Peter Wagner's low stone house.

The morning sun was just touching the tree tops as they walked west the next morning.

A company dressed in homespun sprawled against the stone front of Palatine Church. The militia were part-time soldiers, farmers called from their fields to serve for a few days or a few weeks. Now they must stop the British Army coming from Canada, bent on capturing Fort Stanwix.

They all knew what would happen if St. Leger came back with their Tory neighbors and captured the fort. Nothing could stop the British then. They would sweep down the Mohawk Valley to Albany, burning farms and grain fields. These valley farms, settled a generation before by Palatine Germans, supplied much of the food for General Washington's Army. The fields were now rich and heavy with grain. Without it the American Army would have less to eat the next winter. Starving troops could not fight. The whole war might be lost.

"Tell General Herkimer we're coming," they called to the boys.

"They have to let me join the militia." Jed had talked of little else for many weeks.

"You're near as anything to sixteen," Jan encouraged him. "They took me in the Schenectady Regiment. I said I was going on fifteen."

"You're only thirteen," Jed howled, "though I suppose that is going on fifteen. It's just a further piece than anyone might think. Besides you were the only drummer they could find west of Albany."

By afternoon the heat had sucked all the moisture from the air. Thunder rumbled in the north, but soon a low mutter of sound took its place.

"Look," Jan cried, pointing downhill to the river.

Fort Dayton, a square wooden fort, surrounded by a wood palisade, lay where the West Canada Creek flowed into the Mohawk. The open space around it seethed with movement.

Jed smoothed his homespun shirt and buckskin breeches and retied the thong holding back his brown hair. Jan struggled into the bright blue jacket he drew from his pack.

Jed had never seen anything so exciting. He had to be a part of it. He raced through the gate and up to the door of the blockhouse.

"Whoa up," the sentry called. "You want something?"

"I want to see Colonel Klock. I want to join the militia."

"He's in there with General Herkimer," the sentry replied.

Jed squatted by the door of the blockhouse. His father had joined the Continental line and was marching with General Philip Schuyler to stop the British force coming from Canada by Lake Champlain. Nate, his brother, was too young to fight.

General Herkimer's proclamation had said that two thousand British and Indians had gathered to invade the Mohawk Valley. Everyone from sixteen to sixty was called to active service.

Colonel Klock had to let him join the militia.

Militiamen in homespun and buckskin mingled with a few soldiers in the blue uniform of the Continental line. Outside the fort, along the river, horses nibbled at the grass. Oxen stood placidly in the shallow water and scores of supply wagons stood nearby.

The air was heavy with the odor of animals and cooking fires over which pork and fish were roasting.

CHAPTER TWO

The Army Moves West

Jed scrambled to his feet as Colonel Klock, his father's friend and commander of the Palatine Regiment, emerged from the blockhouse.

"Hello there, Jed," he said. "What are you doing here?"

"I want to join the militia, sir."

"How old are you?"

"Near sixteen, sir. My birthday is in three weeks, on the twenty-fourth."

"Who will look after your farm, boy? General Washington needs all the grain he can get."

"Gramp is there with ma and my brother, Nate, is handy with the horses. Pa took Kaya, the brown mare, and went with General Schuyler. I was born in the valley, sir. I'm an American. If the British aren't stopped, the whole valley will be gone. I want to help."

"You're a good steady boy. I'd like to have you with us." Klock stroked his chin thoughtfully. "Can you read and write?"

"Oh, yes, sir," Jed answered eagerly. "Ma taught me."

"Come then. We'll see what the general has to say."

General Nicholas Herkimer's old blue uniform strained across his chest. His hand, more accustomed to a plough handle, held maps and papers. A Palatine farmer, he must lead his neighbors to stop the British army.

"General," Colonel Klock said, "I think I just found that clerk we need."

"So," the general asked in his strong German accent, "are you a scholar?"

"I can read and write, sir." Jed liked this old man.

"Good. You will be my clerk then and write dispatches and keep my journal."

"Yes, sir. Thank you, sir. And General, I have something to report."

"What is it?"

"Yesterday we saw a Mohawk war party. Only four, but painted. They were going north in a great hurry."

The general looked at Klock, his blue eyes worried.

"So," he said. "Molly Brant is at Canajoharie. Thank you, Jed, you have already helped us. You are dismissed now, but return in an hour."

Jan was waiting outside the blockhouse.

"Did they take you, Jed?" he shouted eagerly.

Jed started an Indian whoop, saw the startled look in the sentry's eyes, and choked it off.

"I'm to be clerk for the general."

"Yahoo!" Jan tossed his drumsticks in the air. "Let's go and catch some fish for supper."

"Say, Jed," he asked later, his mouth full of trout, "what did the general say about the Indians?"

"Only that Molly Brant was at Canajoharie and he was glad to know about the war party."

"Who's she?"

"Joseph Brant's sister. He's the great Mohawk war chief. He'll be at Stanwix with all his warriors to help the British. The Johnsons and the Butlers, our old neighbors from Johnstown, will be there too. They pulled foot for Canada last year but they'll be back now, with all the Tories who used to live in the valley."

8

"I'll drum so loud," Jan promised, "they'll run right back to Canada."

Within an hour Jed was seated at a table in the general's tent.

"We will send a dispatch to General Philip Schuyler," he said, his clay pipe sending out great puffs of smoke. "A bateau goes down river tonight."

Fort Dayton
3 August 1777

General Schuyler:

All are here now except Colonel Visscher and he will come soon. Eight hundred men will march tomorrow for Stanwix. Thomas Spencer, the Oneida and our friend, has followed the enemy from Canada. St. Leger has 1,700 men; 400 regular troops and 600 Tories, our old neighbors. With them come Joseph Brant and 700 Indians.

On the 30th of July, Spencer wrote the Committee of Safety that the King's troops would be at Stanwix in 4 days. Spencer says that if Stanwix surrenders, the Oneidas must withdraw their support.

We march tomorrow to relieve the Fort. I pray they do not surrender before we arrive.

Nicholas Herkimer

There were other dispatches and Jed fought to stay awake. The heat was like a blanket. Lightning flickered in the west but no rain came.

"That is all, boy," Herkimer said finally. "Go to bed now."

Jed stretched his blanket beside Jan who was fast asleep. Before he slept, he thought again of his father and what he had told him of the Committees of Safety, loyal Americans meeting secretly in houses to send messages to the new Continental Congress.

His father had read one such message to him written at a neighbor's house at Stone Arabia. "We are a young country," they had written, "and few in number but not the less attached to American Liberty, united together to defend our Freedom with our Lives and Fortunes."

Jed set his jaw in the darkness. "We'll stop them at Fort Stanwix."

Then he was asleep.

The camp was already stirring as a hot and brassy sun topped the low hills. Horses stamped and whickered as they were hitched to wagons.

Jan drummed the men smartly out of the fort and then took his place in the line near Jed. At the end of the line the oxen plodded along, drawing the supply wagons.

Once when the boys stopped to drink at a stream, Jed climbed a tree and looked back. As far as he could see, a great dust cloud rose above the trees. It was easy to catch up again because the army moved so slowly.

That night they camped at Staring Brook. The boys stowed their gear and went down to the river. It took only a minute to undress and dive into the cool water.

"How far do you think we came today?" Jan asked, as they floated lazily.

"About twelve miles. You can't hurry oxen in this weather."

"Do you think we'll get there tomorrow?"

"No. Not a chance." Jed wished he could talk to Jan

about the general's letter. What if the fort had already surrendered?

That evening Jed sat again in the general's tent. He had waited outside while sounds of an argument came from within.

"Some of my colonels think we move too slowly," the general had said. "They want to march in with drums beating, relieve the fort and be heroes at a banquet, all in one afternoon."

"They don't know about Indians," he went on sadly, "but they will learn. Write in the journal now."

"We have marched twelve miles today from Fort Dayton to Staring Creek and tomorrow we cross and march on the south side. We have had no word from the fort. Colonel Mellen went with two hundred men and supplies last week. The bateaux, which transported them, have not returned. I believe they cannot, as they should be back by now."

"Mark a copy for General Schuyler. Then go to bed."

Jed slept fitfully. In his dreams he saw the fort lost to the British. Indians and Tories streamed down the valley, burning houses and barns, and the grain fields now ripe for harvest.

Lightning flickered again down the river.

CHAPTER THREE

Forward

Tuesday dawned even hotter than the previous day, and the army was on the move earlier.

A tall man, looking very tired, was sitting on a log beside the road.

"That's Adam Helmer," Jed said in amazement. "He can't be resting, he's the best scout in the army. I've heard he can run half a day without stopping once."

"Hello, Adam," he said as they came up. "What's the matter?"

"Hello, Jed," Helmer answered. "Just sat down for a spell, on the general's orders."

"We'll see you in camp." Jed scratched his head, still puzzled as they passed by.

"You'll see me," Helmer promised.

At Oriskany Creek the army stopped for the night and Jed hurried to the general's tent.

"Come," the general said. "We'll go inside."

It was hot inside the tent but Jed figured the general didn't want half the army listening over his shoulder.

Jed looked curiously at the Oneida seated at the table. This was Thomas Spencer, Oneida sachem and fast friend of the American cause.

"Write this down, Jed," Herkimer said. "Spencer just came from Fort Stanwix."

"It was evening when Mellen arrived," Spencer began, "with two hundred men and five bateaux of supplies. Everyone was set to work unloading. While the men and horses were carrying supplies to the fort, Indian campfires were seen in the woods."

"The alarm was sounded," he went on. "Just as the last troops marched into the fort, the British swooped down on the boats. The captain was captured."

"How many king's men?" Herkimer asked.

"A small force that day, but many Indians."

"And the next day, on Sunday?"

"Three officers marched from the king's camp under a flag of truce. Probably to demand that the fort surrender. Presently they marched back again."

"In the afternoon a great sound of drums and fifes announced the approach of the enemy forces."

"I can imagine how they look," Herkimer said bitterly. "The officers, seated on fine prancing horses, will be dressed in their white breeches and bright red coats with gold lace. Behind them will be the king's men and the Hessian mercenaries, eager for battle." After musing silently while waiting for the troops to come into clearer view, Herkimer asked, "Are Indians with them?"

"Out on the flanks," Spencer said. "Nearly a thousand Senecas and Mohawks—war feathers in their scalp locks and their spears and tomahawks shining."

"How many in all, Thomas?" Herkimer asked. "British and Indians?"

They're only trying to scare us off, Jed thought, as his quill scratched away. "They'll find out. Americans don't scare very easily."

"Seventeen hundred," Spencer answered, "maybe more."

Jed hoped neither man heard his quick gasp of breath.

14

"That is bad," said Herkimer shaking his head. "Their entire force has arrived at Stanwix. They are twice as many as we are."

"But," he added, "there are eight hundred men in the fort. That makes it more even."

Jed's hand trembled with excitement. It was hard to write.

"And, now, Thomas?" Herkimer asked. "What happened yesterday?"

"Yesterday," Spencer went on, "the ring was drawn more tightly. Even the bateau men could not leave."

"I thought so," Herkimer replied. "They are settling in to starve the fort into submission. If the fort surrenders, the British can sweep the Mohawk Valley to Albany. Is there more?"

"Today," Spencer said, "I am very worried. All day men have been leaving the British camp. The Mohawks are leaving also. I do not understand it and I do not like it."

The general threw a quick glance at Jed.

"I understand," he said. "Jed saw four painted Mohawks on the trail on Saturday. He thinks they came from Canajoharie."

"So," Spencer's brows drew together. "Molly Brant has sent word of your coming. They do not want you to get to the fort. Watch out for an ambush."

"I shall try," Herkimer replied. "You are our good friend, but you must rest now."

The general smoked his pipe quietly as Jed finished the journal.

"You are a good boy," he said as Jed read the day's entry to him. "I am glad that you have come with us. Now tell the officers that I wish to see them. Tell your friend that he shall be in first to drum us into Fort Stanwix when we get there, but tonight he should sharpen his hatchet."

"He hasn't got a hatchet," Jed began. "He's only thir . . . I shall look after him, sir."

Word of the coming battle had spread through the camp. Men cleaned their guns and sharpened hatchets. Jed wiped his musket carefully and checked his flint box and powder.

"Jed," a soldier called out. "You went up to Stanwix last year transporting supplies with your father, didn't you? What's it like?"

"Swampy," Jed replied. "The fort is between the Mohawk and Wood Creek. Right at the carrying place."

After dark a soldier summoned Jed to the general's tent. He went in and looked with surprise at its only occupant.

"Hello, Adam," he said. "Did you get rested?"

Adam Helmer laughed. "The general wanted me out of the men's sight for a while."

An owl hoot sounded twice outside the tent. Adam went to the opening and admitted two men. In a minute the general came it.

"Good," he said, "we are all here. Did anyone see you, Adam?"

"No, sir."

"I want no one to know until you are well away." The general lit his pipe. "Jed, you will write a letter."

To Colonel Peter Gansevoort, commanding Fort Stanwix:

"We are camped at Oriskany Creek about eight miles from Stanwix. Spencer tells us that you are under siege. We

are 800 men. When these messengers arrive, signal us by the discharge of three cannon. You will know how to keep the enemy occupied from the front. We will attack from the rear. Together I believe we can defeat them."

Nicholas Herkimer

"You will carry the letter, Adam," Herkimer said. "All three of you know the message. Can you get in?"

"Sure." Adam tucked the letter in his hat. "We'll make it."

The three men slipped out and disappeared into the night.

"That is all, Jed. Good night, boy."

"Good night, sir."

The camp was restless as Jed walked carefully back to where Jan had spread their blankets. Men talked in low tones as they huddled over smudge fires.

"How does it look, Jed?" Jan was wide awake tonight.

"Herkimer sent a message to the fort. They will come out and engage the enemy as we attack from the rear."

"Are you scared, Jed?"

"I guess so. I don't want to be but I am. How about you?"

"They don't shoot at drummers, do they, Jed?" Jan's voice quavered a little.

"Only the good ones," Jed managed a chuckle. "You're safe."

Wednesday, August 6, dawned dark, hot and sultry. While the men were cooking their breakfasts, black clouds boiled in the west.

At nine o'clock Herkimer called his officers together.

"We'll get an earlier start this morning." Colonel Cox spoke from his dancing horse, "We're ready to move."

"We'll go soon," Herkimer said.

"What do you mean by soon?" Cox, red faced, demanded.

"Soon," Herkimer repeated. "Last night I learned that yesterday the Mohawks moved out of their camps, as did some British. I figure they are waiting for us between here and Fort Stanwix."

"Good," Cox retorted. "Let's not disappoint them."

"They outnumber us," Herkimer said in a louder voice. "I sent three men to the fort. Gansevoort will fire three cannons as a signal and send his men out. Then we attack."

Cox was screaming. "Now how do we know you sent a message to Gansevoort or maybe to your Tory brother in the British camp. Either you're a Tory, too, or a coward. I'm going to Stanwix. Who's going with me?"

Herkimer jumped into his saddle, wheeled his horse to the west and drew his sword.

"You who talk the loudest," he said to Cox, "be sure you are not the first to pull foot when we see the enemy."

"Drummer," he called.

Jan stepped forward.

"Give them a double roll."

He rose in his stirrups, holding his sword outstretched.

"Forward," he shouted and lowered the sword.

With a great roaring shout, the men grasped their guns and rushed down the road toward Stanwix. It was hard for the wagons to keep up with them.

Jed trotted along, his gun loose in his hand.

"There should be flankers out," he said to himself. "I don't like it."

CHAPTER FOUR

The Ambush

The heat and the swamp soon slowed the first wild rush.

"How far do you think we've come?" Jan asked as they trudged along.

"Two miles, maybe."

"The men think the messengers have been caught."

"They'll make it." Jed wished he felt that confident. "Sneaking through an Indian camp at night would take a long time."

Soon the boys could feel the road dip sharply under their feet. At the bottom of the hill, logs had been placed over a stream to form a rough causeway. On the other side of the stream a level space reached to the opposite steep slope.

"Let's get a drink down there," Jan said. "I'm thirsty."

The first crack wasn't much louder than the sound of a dry stick snapping.

Jed froze. Something terrible was going to happen.

A whistle sounded, loud and shrill, and the west wall of the ravine exploded in steady fire from the enemy hidden there. A solid wave of shots poured down on the men trapped in the ravine.

Jed dove off the causeway pulling Jan with him. The boys crawled behind a log and hugged the ground, burrowing into leaves and dirt.

Jed's blood chilled as Mohawk war cries began at the top of the hill behind them and moved steadily closer to where they lay. Herkimer's army was trapped in an Indian ambush.

Dead and wounded soldiers were all around the boys. Men who had stopped to drink lay with their faces in the water. Groans pierced the din as others tried to crawl to shelter. Indians, with scalping knives and tomahawks, darted in like snakes.

"This way. This way." Herkimer's voice rose above the tumult.

"Over here," he called, urging the men to the plateau.

"We've got to get to the general," Jed shouted to Jan.

The ravine was thick with choking smoke. Jed could barely see Herkimer sitting on his white horse calling to his men. Bullets flew thick as wasps in the space between him and the boys.

"Run for it, Jan," he shouted. "Keep the trees between you and the west slope. The soldiers are better shots than the Indians."

Jan jumped and ran, his drum bobbing up and down on his back.

The Indians coming down the east slope were getting closer. Jed loosened his hatchet, crouched as low as he could, and raced to the plateau.

Herkimer wheeled his horse to the creek to gather any men who survived. Jed heard a musket crack and Herkimer dropped from sight. Jan was already ahead of him racing down hill through a hail of bullets. The old white horse was dead. Herkimer lay beside him, blood coursing from his knee.

"He's dead," Jan sobbed. "The general's dead."

"No, I ain't," the general sat up and roared. "I ain't dead. Not yet. Get me back up that hill."

Jed pulled the general's arm over his shoulder and helped him up the hill. Jan cut the saddle from the horse and hauled it to the foot of a beech tree. Together they lowered the old man onto the saddle. Jan ripped a piece of cloth from his shirt and tied a tourniquet around the wounded leg.

"Good boys," Herkimer leaned back against the tree trunk. "Hand me my pipe."

As though he were sitting on the front porch of his house at German Flatts, Herkimer took out his tinder box and lighted his pipe with the arrow he used for a flint.

"I'll get Dr. Petry," Jan disappeared.

"So far," Herkimer said, surveying the battlefield, "the Indians haven't closed ranks with the Tories. It is our only hope now. If they close their circle, we can't last until our men come from the fort."

"Hark," Jed strained to listen. "The cannon from the fort."

"No," Herkimer replied, "only thunder."

Jan and Dr. Petry came around the beech tree. A bullet had cut across the surgeon's cheek and blood ran down his jaw. His left arm hung limp.

"So," he said to Herkimer. "Let's see what's wrong with you."

"Nothing, nothing," Herkimer replied impatiently. "Bind it up, I have work to do."

"So do all of us who are left." The surgeon motioned to Jan to help him.

"Now," he said when Herkimer's leg was bandaged, "I would like this boy to come with me. He is quick and I cannot work with one hand."

"Take him," Herkimer replied. "We won't need to be drummed into the fort today."

"Jed," Herkimer said, his keen eyes missing nothing of

the battle, "go see what is happening on the east slope the way we came."

Jed crept from tree to tree through the dim woods. Even through the bitter choking smoke he could see bodies everywhere. The woods grew darker as black clouds boiled overhead.

Just ahead he saw a company of Patriots and Oneidas firing muskets and swinging bayonets and tomahawks as they charged the Tories and Indians on the east slope.

Herkimer's deep voice guided Jed back to the beech tree.

"We hold the east hill," he reported. "The men are formed in a circle."

"Good, good," Herkimer replied.

"Captain Diefendorf," he yelled. "I said two men behind each tree. One to fire and the other to strike down any Indian who jumps in with a tomahawk."

The fighting had died to scattered musket shot and an occasional Indian yell. The Mohawks and Senecas chasing the baggage wagons had no appetite to come back. The Indians who remained seemed to prefer to fight on their own rather than taking orders from the British.

Thunder boomed again and reminded Jed of the cannon signal.

"What will happen to us?" he wondered as he watched a thin line of Americans and Oneidas barely holding the east hill. The rest were formed in a circle around the general. Ahead lay the Tories. Behind the patriots loomed the wall of the ravine and the Indians. They could move neither forward nor backward.

"Eleven o'clock," Herkimer said.

Only an hour had passed since they had descended the

ravine. Jed couldn't believe it.

The stillness was frightening. There was no sound except the thunder. No air stirred the trees.

Jed felt his skin crawl. Something was going to happen.

A whistle, loud and clear, broke the silence.

"Stand up to them, men," Jed heard Herkimer shout. "It's
your old Tory neighbors, come back with bayonets."

Jed saw a green uniformed figure coming up the slope
directly at him. At the end of his musket a bayonet glittered.

CHAPTER FIVE

Jed Is Captured

It was David MacDonald from Johnstown. Like most of the Scots settled on their land by Sir William Johnson, they had remained loyal to the British.

Jed raised his musket. How could he pull the trigger? Two years ago he and David had sat together on a quiet spring evening fishing for pike in the Kennyetto Creek.

A rifle cracked behind Jed. MacDonald looked surprised, stumbled and lay still. Cold sweat ran down Jed's forehead.

Up and down the hill old valley neighbors fought hand to hand. Hatchets and bayonets crashed together at quarters too close to musket fire.

Jed lost all count of time. Fresh waves of Tories, swinging their muskets like clubs, rushed the Americans. For the first time, the patriot line wavered.

"Why don't they come out of the fort?" Jed sobbed with exhaustion. "We can't last any longer." Most of the British force was still at Stanwix. The Americans had no reinforcements.

Jed, at the edge of the patriot lines, watched in sick horror as the enemy pushed in the center. For the Americans, the end of the battle was only minutes away.

A deafening crash seemed to push Jed into the ground. The earth shook as though a cannon had been fired in the ravine. Men were flung to the ground as a tall pine exploded into flames. Lightning stabbed the ravine. With a wild roar, the storm, which had been building for days, swept over the armies.

All fighting stopped. Muskets were too wet to be fired. The Tories dropped back into the deep woods while the Americans crawled under trees and rocks.

Jed, crouching under a heavy fir tree, his powder flask tucked inside his shirt, heard someone call to him.

"Over here," he shouted.

Jan, his prized blue jacket smeared with mud and blood, crawled under the branches.

"Jed," his voice quavered. "We'll never get out of here."

"The storm saved us, so far. If only they would come out of the fort to help us. We'll make it, Jan. We have to."

Tree trunks were merely dim shapes through a grey curtain of rain and mist. The air still shook with thunder but there were longer intervals between the crashes. In one of them they heard the general's voice.

"Up here, men," he called.

They joined Herkimer at the beech tree. Men were coming in from all directions. Soaking wet, bloodstained and dirty, more than half of them wore bandages.

"Jed," the general said, "scout back down by the causeway and tell anyone you see to come up. I am preparing a little surprise for the British. When they come back from hiding from that little rainstorm, we shall be up on that low hill over there."

Jed started back toward the west slope. Near where he and Jan had stopped to drink, he saw the body of Thomas Spencer, the Oneida who had warned of just such an attack. Jed wondered if Herkimer knew his friend was dead.

Jed found a small company and relayed the message. As they followed their officers back up the hill, Jed swung to the

right in a circle that would bring him back to the beech tree.

The woods were very still. Jed felt his scalp prickle as though eyes were watching him. He stopped under a tree to listen. Water dripping from its leaves made the only sound.

Like a great leaping cat, the Mohawk dropped out of the tree onto Jed's shoulders. The bear grease smell of the Indian was strong as the oiled body threw him to the ground. Jed went down with a crash that forced the air from his lungs. Wet leaves choked him as he gasped for breath.

Jed thrashed wildly and, with a quick twist, rolled over onto his back. Spitting the dirt from his mouth, he clawed at the Indian. The nearly naked Mohawk was covered with grease and slippery as an eel.

Jed doubled his legs and drove his knees into the Indian's stomach. The Indian grunted and one hand slipped from Jed's shoulder. Jed felt a faint hope. Could he get away before the Indian decided a scalp was less trouble than a prisoner?

The Indian rolled over pulling his tomahawk from his belt. Jed dove like an otter and scrambled up the hill.

The Indian jumped to his feet, rage glittering in his black eyes. Jed raced back across the ravine, leaping over rocks and logs, the Indian so close he could hear his panting breath.

The ravine was steep and covered with underbrush.

With his last burst of strength, Jed gained a few steps on the Indian and dropped behind a log. The Mohawk loomed over him, his tomahawk raised.

Jed threw his hatchet straight at the painted figure. The Indian flung his hands in front of his face as he crashed backward down the hill.

Jed raised his forehead from the spongy log. A violent

trembling shook him and bitter vomit rose in his throat.

There was no time to rest. A great thrashing started at the foot of the hill. The Indian was still very much alive and coming up after Jed as he crawled to his feet and pulled himself to the top of the ravine.

On level ground again, Jed, panting and unsteady, trudged to the American lines. He saw Jan and Dr. Petry first. They were looking for men too seriously wounded to walk. There weren't many. The Indians had seen to that.

"What happened to you?" Jan demanded.

"Indian chased me," Jed answered hoarsely. "Where's the general?"

"Up to the right," said Jan, giving him a sharp look. "He's been asking for you."

It was a little after one o'clock when Jed reported to General Herkimer that the Americans were all out of the ravine.

CHAPTER SIX

The Signal

Jed could see that the Americans were in a better position now. Herkimer's army was not strong enough to advance but they were out of the ravine and ready for the next assault.

It was not long in coming. Across the road poured the green uniforms of Johnson's company. Jed's sharp eyes also noted the painted Indians who were slipping quickly from tree to tree.

If I climbed a tree, Jed thought, I could see what's going on and call down to the general since he can't move.

Selecting a tall pine, he slung his musket on his back and pulled himself up just as the British rushed up the hill toward the Americans. Bullets whistled past his tree and the rush stopped.

The respite was short. Twice as many British poured across the road the next time. Jed squirmed around and looked up the hill. Everywhere the Americans were being pushed back. Jed was behind the British lines now. Soldiers on both sides swung their muskets like clubs as the two armies clashed.

Jed could hardly bear to look. This would surely be the end of the battle. Somewhere soon, the American line would break and the British would pour inside.

I should call back and tell the general, he thought, but what good would that do. He was nearly alone now. The fighting was far behind him.

A rolling boom sounded from the west.

Jed held his breath. They had waited too long.

A second boom. Then a third.

"It's the signal," he shouted wildly. "The signal. They got in!"

His voice barely carried to the struggling Americans, but a ragged cheer broke from the patriot lines. Strengthened by the hope of reinforcements on the way, they fought harder. Slowly the British drew back.

Musket fire rattled down the road.

"They're out of the fort," someone shouted. "They're coming!"

Soon Jed spotted figures marching down the road. They would get to the fort after all.

But why, he thought, squinting his eyes, doesn't it seem right. If only the smoke wasn't so thick.

"It's them all right," a soldier shouted. "you can tell by their brown coats."

Jed could see clearly now. Was he right? He couldn't believe it.

"Stay back," he shouted. "Stay back. They're British."

The marching soldiers were Johnson's Greens. They had turned the uniform coats inside out to resemble the home-spun of the Patriots. They wore hats taken from dead Americans.

Anger gave the Americans new strength and the British retreated down the hill.

A new sound came from across the road.

"Oonah, Oonah," the Indians called.

Could Jed believe his ears? The cry was repeated.

"They've pulled foot," he shouted excitedly. "The Indians are leaving!"

The musket fire slowly stopped. There was not much activity from the British. Jed slid down his tree and went to where the general lay.

"The Indians have all gone, sir," he reported.

"That's good." The general was pale and his voice weak. "And I think our friends across the road are wondering what the sounds from the fort mean. Soon, I think, they will decide to go back and find out."

Within a few minutes he was proved right. The musket fire stopped entirely.

"It's over," Jed thought numbly. "It's all over."

The most seriously wounded were placed on litters. So few officers were left, it was impossible to muster the men.

"We cannot go to the fort," Herkimer said very slowly. "Two hundred or more of our men have been killed and many more were captured. Most of you who remain are wounded. We have lost all our supplies and animals. The enemy still surrounds Stanwix. We will return to Dayton."

"Jed?" Jan's voice quavered. "Haven't we done anything at all?"

"I don't know." Jed looked sadly at the small band of wounded men, remembering the brave army of this morning. "We were supposed to relieve the fort. It's still under siege. I just don't know."

The most able bodied were litter bearers. Others helped the wounded who could walk. There were scarcely enough for either task.

The men were lining up for the march home when Jan, who had disappeared, came up the hill with his drum.

"I hid it," he grinned, "and no one found it."

"Look," Herkimer said. "We are still an army."

Jed stepped between the poles of the general's litter.

"No, Jed," Herkimer said, "come around here. I wish to speak to you."

A soldier took Jed's place and the general's litter was carefully lifted. Dr. Petry spread a blanket over the old soldier's wounded leg.

"A message must go to the fort," Herkimer said. "Colonel Gansevoort must be informed of what happened here today and that the men of the Mohawk Valley will be back."

"Yes, sir." Jed's eyes were smarting. "I have a bit of paper, I can write it."

"No," the general replied. "You are to take the message. You are young and strong and you have been there before."

How can I do it? Jed swallowed a lump in his throat. I'll never make it.

"Tell Gansevoort he must not surrender," the general continued. "The valley must be protected. We will be back. Until then, they must hold on."

"It will not be easy," Herkimer said in a voice that was little more than a whisper. "But you must get in, no matter how long it takes you. Stanwix cannot fall. The valley must be protected. General Washington's Army cannot fight without food. Do you understand, boy?"

"I'll get in, sir," Jed drew a deep breath.

"You are a good boy," the general sighed and his eyes closed.

"Thank you," Jed looked at the pitiful band of men. We never were an army, he thought. We're just . . . people . . . but in a way we won.

"I'll come to German Flatts to see you, sir," he said. "When I get back."

"Here," Jan handed him a linen wrapped package. "Take the rest of the maple sugar. I found some corn to go with it."

"Thanks," said Jed as he tucked the package in his shirt. "Say, Jan, do me a favor."

"Sure."

"Stop at Stone Arabia and tell my folks I'll be home soon."

"Sure. Good luck, Jed."

"Thanks. Same to you."

Jan sounded a roll on his drum. Only a few men could shoulder their muskets. The rest used their guns for crutches.

"All right, boys," the general said, "we're going back down the valley to home."

Jed watched the pitiful little band wind their way through the grey and dripping trees. Long after the last man had disappeared from sight, he could still hear Jan's drum.

Jed blew out his breath in a sigh, straightened his shoulders, and picked up his musket.

"Six miles to the fort," he said to himself. "Better get started."

Jed walked silently on wet leaves, but soon the sun and wind dried the woods. It was harder to be quiet now, and he had to move slowly.

Suddenly his stomach growled. In the tension of the battle, he hadn't felt hunger. Now he remembered he hadn't eaten anything since yesterday.

Looking around he found a heavy thicket. The food packet he took from his shirt was one his mother had tucked into the boys' shirts when they left Stone Arabia. It seemed like something that had happened years before.

As he unwrapped the food, Jed could see the cherry table at home as they sat down for supper. Pa would say grace. For a second after he finished, all you could hear was the crackle of the fire. Then Ma would say, "Amen."

Jed bent his head.

"Bless this food and us to thy service," he said. "And help me to get to the fort. Amen."

He chewed the dried corn moistened with water from his canteen and sweetened with maple sugar. He ate ravenously, watched by the bright eyes of a chipmunk.

"Here," he said, tossing over some kernels of corn. "Don't tell anyone you saw me."

Once out of the thicket, he checked his musket and walked softly toward the fort. Feeling he must be getting closer, he paused and held his breath to listen. Twice there was no sound and he went on. The third time he heard a chink of metal. A breeze from the west brought a faint whiff of smoke.

Jed had been climbing a low hill. The ground was level for a way ahead, then dropped down again. Jed looked about and soon found what he was seeking. A tall pine rose, towering above the shorter growth around it.

Jed summoned all his strength and jumped for the lowest limb. It had looked dead. If it broke, it would sound like a gun shot. His fingers touched the bark, clutched and hung on. The branch held.

Jed pulled himself up until he was kneeling on the branch. The next one looked stronger. Slowly he balanced himself and reached for it.

Soon he was above the tops of the shorter trees and must be more careful. A Tory soldier might see him and Jed figured he didn't look much like a bird.

He was in the crown of the tree now and pulled the heavy limbs aside and peered out. The sight made him draw in his breath and cling to the tree to keep from falling.

Jed was looking straight down into an Indian camp. It

was completely hidden in the fold of the hill. If he had walked for another hundred yards, he would have walked directly into it.

CHAPTER SEVEN

Through the Enemy Lines

The Indians were cooking a partridge. Their oiled bodies shone like polished copper in the firelight.

Jed saw the river off to his right. Next, a little closer to the tree, the road snaked through a narrow swath of clearing. He pulled the branches farther apart.

Jed's heart leaped in his throat. There it was, Fort Stanwix. Directly ahead of him and about a half mile away, its square-shaped outline was sharp and clear in the setting sun. He could see the cannon in their embrasures and the barracks inside the walls.

Tory tents were pitched astride the road not quite halfway between Jed and the fort. It was all just as Spencer had said. The ring around the fort was drawn very tight.

He would have to wait until it was dark. Jed took out the rest of his maple sugar and settled down to wait. He was thinking longingly of his mother's johnny cake and wishing he had a piece, when a movement in the Tory camp set his heart thumping.

Two soldiers marched out. Their smart turn at the road and measured pace confirmed his worst fears. They were patrolling the road.

Jed was nervous and impatient to start. When the first star showed, he climbed down from his perch.

On hands and knees Jed crept forward, testing each spot before he put his weight down. Just the slightest snapping of a twig or the rustling of a leaf would bring the Indians screeching down on the young boy.

A faint glow on his right marked the Indian camp he had seen from the treetop. Jed's heart hammered so loudly he was afraid the Indians could hear it.

He could see a fire now and naked bodies clustered around it. Something was wrong. What was it? Then he knew.

"Why aren't they dressed?" he wondered.

Indians went into battle nearly naked but otherwise wore leggings and shirts of hide. He couldn't understand.

On his left another fire flickered through the trees. He wouldn't be far from either when he crawled through, if he got through. Cold sweat poured down Jed's face.

Not until the last glimmer of firelight had faded, did he dare walk again.

Suddenly all daylight was gone and the woods were totally dark. A low branch plucked at Jed's shoulder. He whirled and crashed into a tree. Lost and nearly exhausted, he stumbled on. The ground grew soft but Jed was running in panic, not realizing he was circling back toward the Indians.

A root caught his foot. Jed pitched headlong into a pool of cold slimy water, but the shock brought him back to his senses. He crawled out and lay trembling on the bank. He had blundered into the swamp. If he could follow along its edge, it would lead him to the fort.

Keeping his hands outstretched, Jed felt his way from tree to tree through a nightmare of underbrush and water. Once he felt dry land all about him and knew he had lost the swamp entirely. He turned sharply to his left, went too far, and plunged into water up to his chest.

Jed pulled himself out and sat with his back against an

old hickory stump.

He was nearly at the end of his strength when a new wave of hope surged through him. He could see the dim shapes of trees silhouetted against a clearing. It could be the fort. Perhaps he has passed the British lines.

Pressing himself against a tree trunk, Jed peered out. Something was terribly wrong. The light colored British tents were still between him and the fort.

Jed leaned against a tree and sobbed. He'd never get in. Dawn was close. As he stood there, the sound of Jan's drum seemed to come to him. Again he could see General Herkimer leading his shattered army back home. Shattered, but not defeated. The British had left the field first.

"What are you going to do?" he said to himself. "Sit here all night? Get going."

Jed stole cautiously to the edge of the woods. Soon the outline of the fort was blotting out more of the sky. He could do it. He'd cross the road just ahead, dash through the meadow and up to the sally port.

Fatigue made him careless. His foot trouched a twig. Jed felt the crunch through his moccasin, tried to pull back, but was too late. It snapped.

"Who's there?" A Tory sentry had heard him.

"Halt," the call came from the road behind him.

Two British soldiers pounded up the road. Jed gave up all attempt at stealth and raced into the woods.

Wind rustled the leaves and made the river slap against the shore. That was the answer. The river. His last chance.

Jed bent over and raced across the clearing. He felt the ruts of the road, more cleared land and then a line of trees. With the sentries close behind him, he plunged into the water.

The noise of the choppy waves would cover his movements and there were cattails to hide his head. The current pushed against Jed's chest as he felt his way along the soft river bottom.

The water was a little deeper at the mouth of a small stream that ran past the sally port. Jed paused. He had hoped to leave the river where the fort loomed directly opposite him, but he didn't dare. The sentries were still too close. The sky seemed lighter. He wouldn't think about that.

Past the fort now, the river began to curve away to the east. Jed crawled up the bank and into a meadow. Settlers had grown hay and wheat here before they fled and there were haycocks scattered about.

At the last haycock now, the greatest danger lay ahead. An American sentry might fire before he could identify himself.

Jed rose to his knees. There was something he should do. He was so tired he couldn't think. Then he remembered, his musket was wet.

Carefully reloading his gun, he primed it and set the flint. With what seemed the last strength in his legs, he raced across the shallow creek and up a low hill. When he stood just outside the sally port, Jed fired his musket.

"Halloo," he called at the top of his lungs. "Messenger from General Herkimer."

"Hurry," Jed shouted. "Hurry. Let me in. I have a message from Herkimer. I'm an American."

He could hear voices inside the fort. Other figures appeared beside the sentry.

"Hurry," Jed was frantic. He could hear the British running across the field behind him. "Hurry. Please."

Commands were shouted and the door began creaking

open. Jed jumped up and raced across the clearing and as the sally port was opened, he ran in. Behind him the sky was light with dawn.

"I have a message for Colonel Gansevoort," he said, as blackness descended upon him.

CHAPTER EIGHT

The Shirt-Tail Flag

"Why didn't Ma call me?" Jed woke to a room bright with sunshine. It must be ten o'clock. What was all that noise outside? He opened his eyes and saw a strange room. The walls were rough boards. He was lying on a narrow cot.

Jed stared at the man sitting beside his bed.

"Adam Helmer," he exclaimed. "What are you . . . ?"

Then he remembered.

"I have to see Colonel Gansevoort," he said, sitting up in bed. "I have to tell him . . . "

"We know you do." Adam pushed Jed back with a firm hand. "The colonel will see you right soon. He's as anxious as you are."

"Hey, there," Adam called out the door. "He's awake."

Jed sank back on the pillows.

A loud boom and a louder crash shook the room.

"What was that?" he asked, sitting up again.

"The British brought some cannon and mortars with them," Helmer answered. "Every little while they throw in some shells so we won't forget they're out there. They don't do much damage unless you happen to be under one when it hits."

"Adam," Jed began. "There was a terrible battle."

A soldier came in carrying a pewter bowl with steam curling from it.

"Here's your breakfast," Adam handed the bowl to Jed.

"Colonel Gansevoort will see him as soon as he finishes," the soldier said from the doorway.

"Good," Helmer answered. "Now get him another bowl."

Finally Jed could eat no more. He got up, washed and dressed in his muddy clothes.

The sun was blinding as they came out of the building. A quick glance showed Jed he had been in the casemates on the south side of the fort. The commandant's headquarters were directly opposite on the north side.

In between there was scarcely room to walk. Seven hundred men overflowed the barracks and camped wherever there was space inside the fort. Supplies were stacked everywhere. The ammunition and other fort equipment were neatly arranged, but here and there piles of blankets seemed to have been dumped in great haste. Jed would have liked to examine them more closely, but they were soon on the other side of the fort.

Colonel Gansevoort's quarters seemed very dim after the bright light outside. A slim man, less than thirty years old, sat behind a table. Jed was surprised at how young the colonel was.

"Jedediah Quackenbush reporting, sir," he said.

Colonel Gansevoort rose and stretched out his hand.

"My congratulations, Jed," he said. "You performed an almost miraculous feat. The enemy knew that Helmer and the others had come in. They must have been particularly on guard."

"Thank you, sir," Jed replied. "The general told me I must get in, sir."

"And like a good soldier you obeyed orders. Sit down, now. Tell me about yesterday."

"We held the best we could," Jed concluded. "In the afternoon it seemed the enemy had enough. After they

46

heard the firing from here, the Indians went off. Then the Tories withdrew."

"That's about it." Jed wanted to ask questions but didn't know whether he should.

"Sir?"

"Yes, Jed."

Jed knew then he would never forget that brave company of Mohawk Valley farmers who stuck cockades in their hats, took their muskets from their cabins, said goodbye to their families and marched off to stop the regular British Army.

"There weren't many left, sir." Jed wished he could tell how he felt about the last glimpse as they went back through the trees to the sound of Jan's drum. "They had to carry the general back home. We didn't get to the fort. Did we . . . did we lose the battle, sir?"

"No, Jed. You didn't lose. I'm not sure yet but the Americans may have won a great victory yesterday. They stopped the British."

"General Herkimer said that reinforcements will come."

"This morning," the colonel continued, "a letter came from American prisoners in the British camp. It said that Americans were defeated, that General Herkimer was killed and that General Burgoyne had captured Albany. None of it seems to be true. I think the British lost many men yesterday. Also many Indians. The Indians do not like being pushed to the front to die in white men's battles. I think St. Leger is very anxious to have the fort surrender before another American army marches up the valley. I think that your Mohawk Valley neighbors struck a great blow yesterday for American freedom. I think the valley will stand firm and General Washington will have the grain for his troops."

"We are grateful to you, Jed, for bringing us the news," the colonel said as he rose from his chair. "If you will wait here a minute, we will have a little surprise for you."

"Adam," Jed demanded. "What happened here yesterday? We heard the signal, then a lot of musket fire and then the cannon."

"It was real interesting," Adam began just as the colonel returned.

"All right, Jed," he said, "come with me."

Outside the door, Colonel Gansevoort motioned to Jed to stand beside him.

The inside of the fort was a hollow square. Bastions, holding the cannon emplacements, jutted out from each corner. Four cannons faced the northwest, three the northeast, and four the southwest. Casemates lined the inside walls with frame buildings in front of them facing the parade ground.

Troops, lined up in companies, nearly filled the parade ground inside the fort.

A drummer stepped forward and began a long roll. The men fell silent and came to attention. The drummer stopped.

"Men," Colonel Gansevoort began, "last night, Jedediah Quackenbush, standing here beside me, came through the enemy lines to bring us news of Herkimer's army. Contrary to the information we received, General Herkimer was not defeated. Our army held the field. It was the British and Indians who ran."

A cheer broke from the troops.

"We would not have known this," Gansevoort continued, "if Jed had not brought us the news. He tells us that reinforcements are coming. We must hold out against the enemy."

There was more cheering.

"Perhaps you have wondered," Gansevoort went on, "why our flag is not flying this morning."

"Flag?" Jed couldn't understand. "What was he talking about? The colonies had no flag."

"Jed," Colonel Gansevoort said, "on Sunday, when Colonel Mellen came in, he brought dispatches and news- papers to the fort. One newspaper told us that on the four- teenth of June, the Continental Congress adopted a flag for the United States."

"A flag," Jed said to himself, in wonder, "we have a flag. I wonder if Jan knows."

Gansevoort went on. "The fort was never supplied with a flag, so we set to work to make one. An ammunition shirt made the white stripes. We had some red stuff but no blue for the field. Then Captain Swartout donated his blue camlet cloak that had been captured at Peekskill. So we made our flag."

"We flew it on Sunday when St. Leger paraded his troops. One of them called to us and asked where we got our shirt-tail flag."

Jed looking straight ahead, saw the tall bare flagpole on the southwest bastion.

"Yesterday," Colonel Gansevoort said, "we were suc- cessful."

Jed could not image what was coming.

"Today," Gansevoort said, "we have something to show the enemy."

A soldier, carrying the folded flag stepped to the base of the flagstaff. Then he turned to fasten the flag to the rope. Jed felt he couldn't wait another minute to see it.

Now, at last, he was ready. The drummer had been

standing with his sticks poised. The roll began as the flag went up the pole.

At the top, the soldier shook it out. The banner waved in the bright August sunlight. Jed couldn't take his eyes from it as the cheers of the men rose from the fort. This was his flag, standing out in the breeze. A shiver ran down his spine.

The soldier shook the rope again. Below the flag were five ensigns.

For a minute Jed could only stare, but the wild cheering told him it was true.

Flying below the Continental flag were five captured British ensigns.

"All right, men," Gansevoort shouted, "back to your stations."

"Thank you, sir," Jed said, hoarsely, "I'll never forget it."

"And we will not forget what you and the men who marched to Oriskany have done," the colonel replied. "When you get home, you can tell your folks that when the American flag was raised here on Sunday, it flew for the first time in the face of an enemy. Today, when it was raised in your honor, it flew for the first time over captured ensigns."

"That's pretty good for a shirt-tail flag," Adam Helmer said.

CHAPTER NINE

Johnny Johnson's Socks

The firing had been dying down all through the flag raising. The cannon stopped entirely and only a few musket shots were heard.

"Tell me about yesterday, Adam," Jed demanded.

"We didn't get in until late in the morning. We had to run across the field to the sally port with the whole British army shooting at us. They're terrible poor shots. We got in and delivered our message. Colonel Willett was mustering the men to go out when the storm broke, and we had to wait. As soon as the rain stopped we went out."

"How many?" Jed asked.

"About two hundred and fifty," Adam continued. "We took one field piece. Willett led us out and we started down the road to meet you people."

"Down that way," Adam pointed to the south. "Then we came to some tents."

"That's the way I came in last night," Jed said.

"We came at the Tories so fast they didn't have time to form up. Most of them were gone anyway. We busted into a tent and . . . hoo . . ." he laughed.

"What is it?" Jed asked.

"You know what a hot day it was," Adam continued, "even after the rain. Here in this tent was Johnny Johnson, Sir John Johnson, Baronet, once the proudest man in the whole Mohawk Valley, taking his ease. He'd taken off his uniform so's he'd be cooler. And . . . and . . . " Adam dissolved in laughter.

"Stop laughing and tell me about it," Jed demanded.

"We busted in," Adam continued, gasping. "And he busted out the back. He was hopping through the brambles like a jack rabbit. Finally he gets to the river and dives in. We let him go."

"When we got back to the tents, Willett sent us to the fort for wagons."

"What for?"

"For the stuff we captured. You never saw so much."

"Didn't they try to stop you?"

"Sure they did, but the Indians were mostly all down in the ravine. The rest ran off as soon as we came."

"So that's where all this stuff came from," Jed remarked looking around.

"That's it. We have seven wagons and they made three trips each. From the Indian camps alone we got a hundred blankets and fifty brass kettles. I don't know how many spears and tomahawks. From the Tory camp we got muskets, ammunition and those flags up there."

"How many men lost, Adam?"

"Not one. They lost some though. Finally old St. Leger pulled himself together and set up a cannon. We had to go back in or we would have been cut off."

"Look here," Adam said lifting the blanket from the pile on which they were sitting. Underneath were scarlet coats, white shirts, breeches, hats and equipment. "This is mine. Take what you want."

Jed didn't know what to say.

"I'll take a red coat," he said. "Nate, my brother, wants one. Say, did any of this stuff come from John Johnson's tent?"

52

"All of it."

Adam watched in amusement as Jed set the red coat aside and burrowed in the pile. Finally he found what he wanted.

"Wait till Gramps sees these," he said gleefully, holding up a pair of socks. "He called after me when I left and said to bring back Johnny Johnson's socks, the ones he ran off to Canada in. Will he be surprised. Thanks, Adam."

"Glad to do it," Adam replied. "Here's a linen shirt. Take that for yourself. Colonel said the bunk you were in this morning is to be yours. You can put your stuff there."

In the evening, Jed climbed to the parapet and looked down at the army surrounding the fort.

"What will happen now?" he wondered.

"All they have to do is stay there." The sentinel on guard seemed to have sensed Jed's unspoken question.

"How can we hold out?"

"I don't rightly know," the soldier answered. "We had food for about four weeks. One week's gone by. With the ammunition we captured we'll be all right for the small arms, but there's only enough powder for nine rounds a day on each cannon."

"The reinforcements will come," Jed said. "All we have to do is hang on."

"I hope you're right," the soldier said. "It's certain we can't fight our way out, but I ain't so sure they won't try to fight their way in."

Jed spent the next day exploring the fort. The enemy was quiet. A few shells came in but did no harm. The cannon at the fort answered. Captured equipment was put away. The soldiers were eager to hear of the battle at Oriskany and Jed was kept busy answering questions.

Just before supper one afternoon, Jed was leaning on the parapet looking at the Mohawk. A log floated by.

"In a couple of days," he said to himself, "that log will be by Fort Plain, only a few miles from Stone Arabia. Wouldn't it be funny if Nate and Gramps were down with the grain and saw it."

Across the river the Hessians were cooking supper on their fires.

"They're Germans too," Jed thought, "like Gramps." His grandfather had often told him how he had come from Germany with others from the Palatine section after a drought had destroyed their farms. He described how they had cleared the rich Mohawk Valley farmland on which the grain now grew yellow and heavy. Both Jed and his father had been born on that farm. Even Gramps no longer had any ties with the old country.

"How can we ever win this war?" Jed looked at the Hessian camp. "They're trained soldiers paid by the English King, but we stopped them at Oriskany. We farmers stopped them. Maybe that's why. We're fighting for our own farms, our own land, our freedom. They don't really care. They're not fighting for anything. Even the Tories, they're fighting more against us than for anything."

A shout from the sentry interrupted his thoughts.

"Ho," he called, "movement at the British camp."

Out from the line of tents stepped a drummer. Clad in a brick red coat, he held his drum sticks poised in readiness until his companions motioned they were ready to march.

Behind him, marching toward the fort, was a soldier carrying a flag staff. On it flew a white flag.

"What is it?" Jed asked.

"A flag of truce," the sentinel answered. "Someone is

coming."

Three officers marched across the open meadow behind the flag. The men at the fort were silent.

Beneath the fort, they stopped. One of the men stepped forward.

"We have a message for Colonel Gansevoort," he said.

"From whom?" said the colonel from atop the parapet.

"From Barry St. Leger, Brigadier General of His Majesty's forces."

"Very well," Gansevoort said. "Ensign, blindfold them and bring them in."

CHAPTER TEN

We Demand That You Surrender

"Here they come."

Soldiers crowded the ramparts to see the enemy.

An orderly hurried about the fort, speaking to the officers. One by one they went to the commandant's headquarters.

"Lieutenant Helmer, sir," the orderly said, approaching Jed and Adam. "Colonel Gansevoort requests that you come to his quarters. And er . . . Mr. Quackenbush, you also."

For a startled moment Jed looked around to see who was standing behind him.

"Well!" Adam exploded in laughter. "May I accompany you, Mr. Quackenbush?"

"Please be seated, gentlemen." Gansevoort indicated three empty places near him at the table.

The room was dark and hot. Tightly closed shutters on the windows would give the enemy no glimpse of the fort's defenses. Candles burned in a silver candelabra on the table.

"We will hear you now," he said. "May I ask who is to speak?"

One of the scarlet coated officers rose.

"Colonel Gansevoort," he said, "I am Major Ancrom, adjutant to Colonel St. Leger. I have been directed to speak for him."

"St. Leger was a Brigadier General a minute ago," Jed whispered to Adam. "Don't they know what he is?"

"General St. Leger has directed me to inform you," the

major continued, "that, so far, he has been able to restrain the Indians. With great difficulty he has persuaded them to agree that they will harm no one if the fort surrenders. All officers and soldiers will be allowed to keep their baggage and personal property."

"I am also directed," Ancrom continued, "to remind you that Herkimer died at Oriskany and his army is defeated. There is no hope or relief from that quarter."

"Humph," Jed grunted, nudging Adam.

"There is no hope of relief," Ancrom continued. "Burgoyne is now at Albany. Sooner or later this fort must fall into our hands."

"That can't be true," Jed told himself. "It must be another lie. General Schuyler would have stopped Burgoyne before Albany. If that's true, then Schuyler has been defeated . . . and . . . Pa's dead . . . and Kaya . . . ."

He wrenched his thoughts back.

"General St. Leger hopes that these terms will not be refused," he was saying. "If they are, the general will not be able to restrain the Indians. They are threatening to march down the country and destroy the settlements."

He sat down. Excited conversation buzzed through the room.

Colonel Willett rose to his feet. The room became quiet.

"You have made a long speech," he said. "It amounts to this. If the commandant of the Garrison does not surrender this fort, your general will send his Indians to murder our women and children. Tell him we have been charged with the defense of this fort. We will do our duty."

Jed nudged Adam and grinned.

"When you get outside this fort," Willett said, looking straight at Ancrom, "you may turn and look at it from the outside, but do not expect to come in again except as a prisoner."

Half an hour later the British had returned to their camp.

That evening Jed was standing at his favorite place on the parapet when Adam climbed up and stood beside him.

"Jed," he said, in a low voice, "come over here where I can talk to you. The colonel said I could tell you but he doesn't want the men to know yet."

"What is it?"

"We have to get word out of the fort. No one knows whether we've surrendered or whether we're all dead for that matter."

"That's right," Jed agreed. "Are you going out?"

"This is the plan," Adam said. "Colonel Willett and another man are going out. They will go to Albany and report to the committee. If the militia has not already been raised, they will call it out."

"The fort can hold out until he comes back with reinforcements," Adam went on. "If General Herkimer is on the way back, so much the better."

"What about you?" Jed asked.

"Colonel Willett has to get out," Adam continued. "So if someone went out of the fort and seemed to be heading north and made just enough noise to give the Indians and British something to think about, two other men might be able to slip out to the south, don't you think?"

"You'll be able to find out about Burgoyne, too."

"That's right. Look after my stuff while I'm gone. I'll stop at Stone Arabia and tell your folks you're sitting in the fort, doing nothing and getting fat."

"Thanks, Adam," Jed replied. "I reckon I'll still be here when you get back."

"I reckon you will, Mr. Quackenbush," Adam laughed as he climbed down and crossed the parade to the commandant's quarters.

Jed heard shots in the night. He went to the window to listen but they did not continue.

"Don't let it be Adam," he thought as he fell asleep again.

The next morning, Jed had been watching a soldier from Boston carve a ship's hull from a block of pine when the drum summoned them. The men assembled on the parade as Colonel Gansevoort emerged from his quarters.

"We have received a formal demand for surrender," he said. "This is our answer."

> *Fort Stanwix*
> *August 9, 1777*

Sir:

Your letter of this day's date I have received in answer to which I say that it is my determined resolution with the forces under my command, to defend this fort to the last extremity in behalf of the United American States who have placed me to defend it against all their enemies.

> *Peter Gansevoort*

"The answer goes immediately," he said. "I expect the truce of the past few days will end very soon."

No sooner had the messenger returned from the British camp and entered the sally port when a shell burst from the British cannon. Soon the fort shook with constant explosions. A shell went through the barracks roof, but no one was hit.

Colonel Gansevoort ordered all provisions and supplies removed from the barracks in case of fire. The fort's papers

61

and paymaster's books were put in the safer southwest bastion.

The shelling continued all night. Jed lay in his bunk, unable to sleep as the fort shook and explosions rattled the walls. It continued without interruption until daybreak.

The enemy was determined to capture the fort.

CHAPTER ELEVEN

The Siege

The fort was quiet when Jed awoke.

"It's Sunday," he thought. "Just a week since Jan and I joined Herkimer at Dayton."

There was little activity at the fort. During the morning Colonel Gansevoort assembled the men. He read some verses from the Bible and offered a prayer for the United States. After the brief services, the men sought what rest they could get.

The day remained quiet. Colonel Gansevoort asked Jed to help sort and list the captured British papers. He was working in the colonel's quarter when he heard shouting outside.

"Fire!" someone yelled.

Smoke was billowing up outside the walls. A strong wind blew it across the fort.

By this time a shower of sparks was falling inside the fort. Soldiers grabbed coats and blankets to beat them out. Several lodged in the barrack's roof and small tongues of flame flickered.

"Get water," an officer shouted. "If the fire gets to the powder magazine, we'll all be blown to bits."

Guards were stationed at the east parapet and the sally port was opened. Water-filled buckets were passed from hand to hand from the stream to the rapidly burning roof. Luckily the fire was brought under control and was out soon.

Jed went back to headquarters to continue his work.

In a few minutes, Colonel Gansevoort came in with some other officers.

"What did you think of that?" Colonel Gansevoort asked.

"I think they hoped the barracks would set fire to the powder magazine," one said.

"That's right," Gansevoort agreed. "A fire there would blow us apart."

"I believe our reinforcements are coming," another said. "They wanted to blow up the fort before they have to pull out."

"I think that is what they would like to have us believe," the first said. "They won't go."

By sunset no army had come. The British bombardment began again and continued until a heavy thunderstorm put an end to the firing.

The next day was quiet. Very few troops were seen and there was almost no firing. Many felt that the reinforcements were very near.

"It's just the way it was last week," a soldier said to Jed. "When you folks were coming."

But no reinforcements appeared. The next morning Jed realized with a start that it was Wednesday and he had been in the fort a whole week. What had happened? Surely the army would come tomorrow.

After that, one day seemed the same as another. There was no longer any talk of reinforcements.

Jed had been in the fort for more than two weeks when an orderly came to tell him the colonel wished to see him.

What can it be? he wondered as he walked across the fort. The work on the captured papers had been completed many days before.

Inside the commandant's headquarters, Colonel Gansevoort and several Mohawk Valley men were seated around the table.

Jed took an empty place. After a few more had come in, Colonel Gansevoort sighed deeply and rose to his feet.

"Gentlemen," he said, "we have come to a hard decision. On this coming Sunday, the twenty-fourth . . . "

"Hey, that's my birthday," Jed thought. "I'd forgotten all about it."

"On the twenty-fourth, this fort will have been under siege for four weeks. Two weeks have gone by since Colonel Willett left the fort. Two days ago I sent Lieutenant Nellis out to meet Willett. No one has returned."

"I pledged to hold this fort," he went on solemnly. "We have held it as long as possible. Our food is nearly exhausted, our powder gone. We can hold the fort no longer."

"You men have been summoned because you know the country between here and Fort Dayton. More than half of the soldiers are from Massachusetts. They could not find their way to safety."

"We will not surrender," Gansevoort went on. "We will fight our way out. Those who get away will be able to join the American forces. General Washington needs every man. We will be free men or die here."

He paused for a minute, looking much older than his twenty-eight years.

"I shall lead the charge from the fort," he continued. "After we are through the enemy lines, the responsibility will be yours. The men will be divided into small companies. You men will be guides. It will be your responsibility to get your company to Fort Dayton. I realize that I am asking the impossible. I ask it in the name of our Republic, the United States, which needs every man."

This time he paused so long that Jed thought he had finished.

"We can wait no longer," he said at last. "We will go out tomorrow night."

CHAPTER TWELVE

The Deserter

Jed had packed the scarlet coat and socks in a knapsack and was sorting through the things Adam had left when Handyfoot Folts, an old valley neighbor, entered the barracks.

"They're going to start distributing the food packets at noon," he said. "I'd hoped we could hold out a mite longer."

"How will you go tonight?" Jed asked.

"Cross the river as soon as I can and make a run for it," he answered. "You can't be quiet with a whole company of soldiers. I aim to get them on the road and move fast."

British shells were shaking the fort every few minutes.

"Handyfoot?" Jed rubbed his hand over his face and sighed, "Do you think . . . ?"

He didn't know how to say it.

"Don't think about it, boy," Handyfoot said. "After all, you got in when no one thought you could do it. It's a day the same as any other. Some will get through and some won't. It's best not to think about it."

"The bombardment is letting up," he went on. "It must be time for St. Leger to take his morning nap."

Jed climbed the parapet to study his route for tonight. He'd do his best. That was all he could do.

"Hey. Look over there." The sentry pointed to the British tents. "Something is going on."

There seemed to be great activity at the British camp. Men were running from tent to tent and war whoops sounded from the woods.

"Go down and ask the colonel to come up here, will you? I don't like the looks of that. Looks like an attack to me," he continued as Jed hurried down.

When Jed returned with the colonel, there were fewer British soldiers in sight.

"They must be preparing for an attack," Colonel Gansevoort said. "They're probably making up their formations in the woods. Double the guard. Alert the men."

The drummer beat the call and men scrambled to the parapet until the fort bristled with guns.

Jed peered toward the completely deserted camp. How strange it looked.

"Look," he said, "there's a man in the trenches. What is he doing?"

The sentry raised his gun but the man was protected by the zigzag trenches.

"I'll get him in a minute," the sentry said.

"Wait," the colonel ordered. "He's waving something. Don't shoot."

"It's a white shirt," someone said.

"It's a white flag," another shouted. "He wants to come in."

"Who are you?" the colonel called. "What do you want?"

"I want to join you," the man was closer now.

"A deserter," Gansevoort said. "Let him in but be careful."

The man shouted something else. It sounded like Bennington.

"I couldn't have heard right." Jed didn't dare believe what he had heard.

The sally port had been opened. A wild cheering rose.

"Burgoyne has been defeated," the men yelled, slapping each other on the back. "Burgoyne has been defeated."

"Back to your stations," Gansevoort roared. "It may be a trick. Get back on the parapet and keep your guns ready."

"Let's hear your story," he said to the red-coated soldier. "Who are you?"

"John Cross, sir. I was forced into the army, sir."

"What about Burgoyne?"

"A message came yesterday," Cross said. "There was a battle at a place in the New Hampshire Grants. Bennington, they called it. Burgoyne lost a thousand men and all his supplies."

"Why did you come to us?" Gansevoort demanded.

"I had my passage to come to America to live when I was forced to join the army. Once before I tried to desert, but I was caught. Then this morning, in all the confusion . . . "

"What confusion?" Gansevoort demanded.

"The British are running, sir."

"What?"

"I thought you could see them from the fort. St. Leger and his men are running back to Canada."

"Wa-hoo." Before the war Jed had hunted and fished with Indian boys who had taught him how to sound a war whoop. Jed quickly stepped behind a tall soldier.

"Fire the cannon," Gansevoort ordered. "We'll see if there is any truth in this."

Matches were touched to the fire holes and cannon balls arched toward the British camp.

The fort was silent as every man waited.

The boom of the American cannon echoed from the trees. There was no other sound.

"Why are they leaving?" Gansevoort looked puzzled.

"I don't know," John Cross answered. "This morning all the officers hurried to St. Leger's tent. I had been sent out for firewood when I heard shouting and saw the men running. I hid until they were gone. Then I came here."

"Ho," a sentry called. "Someone else from the British camp."

Another man was running across the field.

Jed looked at him intently. He looked somewhat familiar, but the distance was still too great. Then he was around the corner of the fort and out of Jed's sight.

The man was brought before the colonel but something was wrong. He only hung his head and remained silent. Jed forgot about his war whoop and stepped out for a closer look. The man saw the movement and looked up.

"Jed," he called. "Jed. General Herkimer's dead. Did you hear that, Jed. Old Honikol's dead."

Tears stung Jed's eyes. Once more he saw the old general sitting under the beech tree and then the silent march through the grey woods.

"Jed," General Gansevoort called. "Do you know this man?"

"Yes, sir." Jed jumped down to the parade ground. "That's Hans Yost Schuyler. His mother is General Herkimer's sister. He worked with us last year on my father's bateau."

"Did the general get back home?" Jed asked Schuyler.

"Yes, Jed. He died in his bed reading his Bible."

"I'm glad he got home. Even for a little while."

"A very great loss," Gansevoort said. "I'm sorry he never knew that he helped save Stanwix after all."

"What about this man?" someone shouted. "He's British. He's a spy."

"Colonel, sir," Jed spoke carefully. "Hans Yost is a good

70

man but sometimes his mind gets mixed up."

"Very well, Jed," the colonel said. "You talk to him. Find out what he knows about Cross' story."

"Hans," Jed said slowly, "where did you come from just now?'

"From the camp, over there," Hans Yost waved to the British camp.

"Tell me, Hans Yost," Jed asked, "where are St. Leger and John Johnson and all the men?"

"Gone back to Canada, Jed. Running through the woods with the Indians chasing them."

"Hans," Jed asked very slowly, "do you know why the British are running?"

"Sure I do," Hans grinned vacantly.

"Why did they go, Hans?"

"Because I told them to . . . hee . . . hee," he giggled.

The men in the fort shuffled their feet and looked at each other. How could anyone believe this half-wit?

"Thank you, Jed," Gansevoort said. "I guess that's all."

"Colonel, sir," Jed stammered, "I know Hans Yost. He's odd but I've never known him to tell a lie."

"Very well, Jed," the colonel said. "Go on."

"Hans," Jed continued, "who shot those holes in your coat?"

"General Benedict Arnold, himself, Jed."

The fort exploded in laughter. Men choked and gasped as tears rolled down their cheeks.

"Please, Colonel Gansevoort," Jed pleaded. "I believe he is telling the truth. I think all the men confuse him."

"Jed," Colonel Gansevoort said, "as long as I've been a soldier, I've never come onto anything like this before. Come into my quarters. We'll see if we can make any sense of this."

"Keep double guard," he ordered. "If this is a trick, they will come soon."

CHAPTER THIRTEEN

How Many Stars in the Sky

"All right, Jed," Colonel Gansevoort said, when they were seated, "find out all you can."

"Hans Yost," Jed said, "tell us everything that happened."

"Walter Butler went out of the British camp. He went down the valley to get reinforcements."

"That's right," Cross broke in. "After you refused to surrender, St. Leger sent a proclamation to the people of the Mohawk Valley asking them to join the Royal forces."

"Hans," Jed asked, "why did you go with Butler?"

"I wanted to see my mother and my sister."

"Go on. What happened?"

"Mr. Butler made a great long speech at Shoemaker's Tavern, near Fort Dayton. There were some Tories there. The shutters were all closed and it was very hot. Mr. Butler told them that they must persuade the Americans to give up and join with him. Right in the middle of it, a company of American soldiers came in and captured us. They took Mr. Butler and me away."

"Where did they take you?" Jed asked.

"To Fort Dayton. General Benedict Arnold was there."

"We were tried as spies," Hans Yost said. "Mr. Butler and me. Colonel Willett sentenced us to be shot."

"Colonel Willett," Gansevoort shouted.

"Please, Jed," Hans said. "I didn't mean no harm."

"That's all right, Hans," Jed wanted to shout too. "You have brought us very good news."

"We were supposed to be shot," Hans Yost continued, "but some American soldiers had known Mr. Butler in Albany when he was in law school there. So they talked about it and they decided to put him in prison instead. They took him away."

"What about you?" Jed asked.

"I didn't go to school anywhere, Jed. They were still going to shoot me. My coffin was made. I saw it. Then my mother came to see General Arnold. My brother Nicolaus came too. You remember them, Jed."

"Nicolaus and his mother are both loyal Americans, sir," Jed explained. "I don't think Hans Yost understands about the war."

"My mother talked to General Arnold," Hans Yost said. "They talked for a long time. Finally General Arnold agreed to let me go if I would do something."

"What was that?" Jed asked eagerly.

"They would let me go if I came back to the British camp and told them a big story and made them run away. I didn't want to do it, Jed."

"Why not? Were you afraid?"

"No, not of them, but my mother always said she would beat me if she ever caught me lying. This would be an awful lie, but she said I should do it. She told General Arnold she would stay as a . . . a . . . "

"Hostage?" Jed supplied.

"That's it. General Arnold said he would keep Nicolaus instead."

"They took my coat and General Arnold himself shot holes in it," Hans Yost said proudly.

"I came into the camp this morning. On the way up I met three Oneidas and I told them about the trick. I knew they would help me. Indians love tricks."

"The Indians like you, don't they?" Jed said.

"Yes," Hans Yost answered. "I like them, too. I used to hunt with them all the time. Sometimes I stayed in their villages. They would ask me when it was going to storm or how much game we would see."

"I went to the Mohawk camp first this morning," Hans Yost continued. "They were holding a council. They wanted to go back to Canada. I showed them the holes in my coat and they were very excited. I told them I had been captured by the Americans and they had shot at me when I escaped. I told them I had rushed to tell them that General Arnold was coming with many troops. They asked how many. I pointed to the leaves on the trees. Can Hans Yost count the leaves on the trees? I asked them. That is how many troops are coming with General Arnold."

"They were terribly excited. They went to tell Colonel St. Leger and he sent for me."

"What did you tell him?" Jed's heart was beating so fast, he could hardly talk.

"I told him General Arnold was coming with two thousand troops. I told him I had been caught and condemned to die. I said they were going to hang me and when I saw the gallows, I decided I did not want to be hung and that I would rather take a chance of being shot. I told him I had escaped."

"While I was talking to St. Leger," he went on, "the three Oneidas came into the Mohawk camp. They said a great bird had appeared to them and told them important news. Warriors were coming in great numbers and they had come to warn their Mohawk brothers."

"St. Leger tried to stop the Indians. He called John Johnson to his tent. Do you know something, Jed?" he said, "I think St. Leger is afraid of Indians."

"The Indians started leaving right away. They packed what was left of their belongings and ran through the British camp. Some of the British soldiers thought the Indians were after them," Hans Yost smiled. "The Indians were screeching real loud."

"Soon the British were running too. They didn't take time to pack anything. Then a couple of Indian chiefs began yelling, 'they're coming, they're coming,' the British even threw away their guns and knapsacks. The Indians thought it was a fine joke. They have all gone."

"That's all, Jed," he said. "General Arnold won't shoot Nicolaus now, will he?"

"No, Hans," Colonel Gansevoort said, "you did very well."

When they went out to the parade, men were coming in the sally port, carrying heavy loads of muskets.

"It's all true, sir," Captain Jansen said. "They've gone. You never saw anything like it. They left everything. Tents, blankets and food still cooking in the pots. There is a trail of knapsacks all the way to Wood Creek. They're on the way to Oneida Lake now. They even left eight new bateaux behind at Wood Creek."

"I brought this, sir," Jansen said as he indicated a dark wooden case, trimmed with silver, which one of the soldiers was carrying. "It's St. Leger's writing desk. All his papers and orders are in it."

"Thank you, Captain," Gansevoort said. "I doubt if he'll have any further need for them."

Jed walked slowly about the deserted British camp, remembering the night he had first seen it. Tents stood in orderly rows. Ammunition was stacked by the cannon. Dress uniforms awaited the day their owners planned to march in triumph down the streets of Albany.

The horses were put to work moving the captured cannon. Everyone worked until sunset but there was much left to do.

Major Cochran's party returned with four prisoners.

"It's all just as Hans said," he reported. "They are still running in panic. They have no guns or food and only the clothes they are wearing. The Indians are really enjoying it. St. Leger expects to be scalped at any minute."

"Men," Colonel Gansevoort said, as they assembled at sundown, "we give thanks tonight to God who has preserved us. We remember General Herkimer, who died for the cause of freedom and all the others who fell at Oriskany. Tonight a captured British cannon will fire the sunset salute to the American flag."

The cheers of the men nearly drowned out the sound of the cannon.

CHAPTER FOURTEEN

In the Name of the United States, I Salute You

Saturday was spent bringing equipment into the fort and sorting it. Jed was set to work on a huge quantity of captured papers.

Sunday morning saw even more activity in the fort. Since the men from Massachusetts were leaving with General Arnold, they were busily packing their gear. Although the danger from the north had lessened with the retreat of St. Leger and his men, the threat had not disappeared completely. The Americans feared that St. Leger's troops might be resupplied and reinforced and return to attack again. The fort would continue to be garrisoned by Colonel Gansevoort and his men and a portion of General Arnold's army. The men who were to remain were busily checking their weapons, ammunition and other supplies. They wanted the fort to be well prepared in case another attack should come.

The sun was shining on the American flag as it rippled in the morning breeze. The six captured British ensigns floated below the flag today, for St. Leger's had been added.

Jed leaned on the parapet.

"I'll be home in a few days," he thought, eagerly. "What a lot I'll have to tell them."

"Ho," a sentry called.

Without thinking, Jed looked toward the deserted British camp.

"To the south," the sentry shouted.

Jed ran around the ramparts until he was standing under the flag on the southwest bastion. He climbed to the top of the parapet and crooked his arm around the flag staff. Holding onto the staff, he leaned far out and peered to the south. He could feel the flag rippling over his head.

There was movement far down the road. Sun glinted on metal. Now he could hear a distant drum beat.

They moved so slowly that for a long time it seemed to Jed there was no movement at all. Then they came around the last bend in the road and were marching toward the fort. Wild cheering broke from the throats of the men in the fort.

In the lead a drummer in the uniform of the Continental line beat a steady roll. His uniform was spotless and his drum sparkled in the sun.

"Jan," Jed shouted, happily, waving his hat. "Jan."

Jan grinned broadly, tossed his sticks in the air and caught them without missing a beat.

Around the fort the cannon began to boom the salute to the troops, one . . . two . . . three.

Behind Jan a soldier in blue and red was carrying a flag made of silk. The red and white stripes sparkled. The stars seemed to glitter on their field of blue.

"It's beautiful," Jed thought, "but ours has been in battle."

Four . . . five . . . six . . . the cannon sounded.

Behind the flag rode General Benedict Arnold. He lifted his hat in salute to the men who lined the walls and the flag that flew over their heads. His horse pranced, making the general's sword reflect the sunlight.

Seven . . . eight . . . nine . . . ten cannons spoke. Captured British cannon were saluting now.

"Jed," a voice called from the group of officers riding

behind the general.

"Pa!" Jed called, "Kaya!" The brown mare pricked her ears.

Behind the officers, the men marched smart and proud. Some of them wore the uniform of the line, but many were in their ordinary clothes. The Mohawk Valley men of Oriskany had come back.

General Arnold's army lined up on the field outside the fort and stood at attention as Colonel Gansevoort led his men out of Fort Stanwix. Arnold's color bearer dropped their flag in salute.

Jan beat a loud roll on his drum as General Arnold dismounted and stopped in the middle of the field between the two groups of soldiers.

"On behalf of General Washington, our commander in chief," he said, "I wish to offer the thanks of the American Republic to the men who fought at Oriskany and the men who defended Fort Stanwix. News of this victory will inspire the troops now camped above Albany. Our army, which is nearly fifteen thousand men, will soon stop Burgoyne's advance."

"The British, who considered themselves our masters, have learned a lesson at Oriskany and Stanwix. They have learned that Americans do not recognize masters. When they came to this fort to demand surrender, they expected to be obeyed. They learned that we truly believe that all men are created equal and that each has a right to choose his own course."

"I do not doubt that you men, choosing to be free or die in the attempt, have struck a mighty blow to establish the independence of the United States and to secure the liberties for which we stand."

"In the name of the United States, I salute."

Colonel Gansevoort acknowledged the salute as the men cheered themselves hoarse.

"Jan! Pa!" Jed raced across the field.

"Happy birthday, Jed," they both said together.

"I forgot," Jed rubbed his cheek against Kaya's soft nose. "It is my birthday. I'm sixteen."

"Sure," Jan said. "Now you can join the militia."

Burgoyne was defeated at Saratoga. On October 17, 1777 his entire army laid down their arms in surrender.

St. Leger never returned to the Mohawk Valley.

Lord Howe sailed with his army for Chesapeake Bay.

The bold plan of the British failed completely. This defeat of the British Regular troops by continentals and militia marked a turning point in the American Revolution, made the French our allies, and helped assure the independence of the new Republic.

Katherine M. Strobeck lives in Amsterdam, New York and was graduated from Amsterdam Public Schools and Mt. Holyoke College. She was formerly Supervisor of Guidance in the Amsterdam school system and owner of Amsterdam Lumber Company. A past president and a continuing active member of the Montgomery County Historical Society and an Honorary Member of the Board of the Charleston Historical Society, Miss Strobeck's other memberships include the Amsterdam Chapter DAR, the Schenectady Historical Society and the Broadalbin-Kennyetto Historical Society. She has held the position of the Town of Amsterdam Historian for twenty years.

Previous books are *Mohawk Valley Happenings* and *Port Jackson, An Erie Canal Village*. Other publications include "Strange Childhood" in the *Yorker*, published by the New York State Historical Society; "The Canal Built by Amateurs" in *North Country Life*; the poem, "Promises" and articles in Chapbooks of Maine Writer's Conference, Ocean Park, Maine.